is 35 inches for men and 33 inches for women. For many golfers, this is too long, as it impedes a proper pendulum stroke. A better choice for many players is a club between 31 to 34 inches, a length that

allows the arms to hang naturally and swing freely. New trends are presenting golfers not only with shorter putters, but also much longer options. Longer models are based on new putting tech-

niques that us the sternum, o fulcrum for th These long pu just over 40 to well over 50 inches in length.

for your poor putting. Many of the greatest putters, including the master of the greens Ben Crenshaw, have stayed with the same putter for many years. They know it is not the putter, but the person wielding it that makes the difference.

Putter Styles at a Glance

The blade putter with the shaft attached at one end of the head, is the classic putter shape, in existence since the beginning of golf. The center-shafted or bullseye model has the same thickness from heel to toe. The offset model enables the hands to be visually positioned ahead of the ball and generally is heel/toe weighted. The mallet shape with its large D-shaped head has the advantage of being well balanced even on off-center hits.

Classic blade

Center-shafted with face insert

Offset head

Mallet head

The Putting Stroke

For many golfers, the search for a solid putting stroke is virtually never-ending, involving almost constant tinkering, adjusting, and refining. There are probably as many different strokes as there are golfers, and there is no clear-cut right or wrong. Success is the final measure. If it works, it's right!! But many of the best strokes share certain characteristics. These are highlighted in the following stroke sequence.

1 **Set-up** Ideal set-up position is marked by a comfortable stance and posture, with shoulders square to target line and hands level with or slightly ahead of the ball. Eyes are over the target line and the ball is positioned forward of the eyes, just inside left heel.

2 **Backswing** Arm, shoulders and putter move back in a one-piece action. The hands remain inactive and the head remains steady. The putterhead is kept close to the ground.

Putting Tips

on the GO
What You Need to Know

USGTF
UNITED STATES GOLF TEACHERS FEDERATION

Choosing a Putter

Nearly 50 percent of strokes during a round occur on the putting green. Although developing a feel for the speed of the greens through the use of an effective stroke is by far the most important factor in solid putting, finding the putter that suits your size, stroke, and particular feel can make a huge difference. With the explosion of styles and materials on the market, trying to find the right putter can be daunting. Never buy a putter without first trying it out, preferably during a round. Here are a few essential things to consider in making a decision.

The Putterhead

In terms of weight, balance, and surface quality, there have been many design innovations involving the putterhead. Heel/toe weighting, also known as perimeter weighting, is a technology that helps keep the putter on-line through the stroke. It is accomplished by making the center of the putter much thinner or by including face plate inserts of a lighter material. Putterfaces may also be milled to ensure an extremely flat surface. The aim here is to increase the consistency of the way the ball comes off the putterface. Variables such as the state of the green may, in fact, offset any real benefits from such delicate improvements.

The hosel

The hosel is the part of the club where the shaft connects to the head. The two standard varieties are shown at left: The straight or "bullseye" hosel (on left) is ideal for a player who aligns his hands directly over the ball at address. The offset hosel next to it is better for players whose hands are slightly ahead of the ball at address.

Length

The standard putter length

Note: Most of the instructions in this book assume a right-handed address. If you're left-handed, simply reverse the instructions.

2

3 Completion of backswing Head and legs have not moved, wrists remain unbroken and putter is still close to the ground.

4 Through impact Arms and shoulders bring putterhead back along the same path as the takeaway and into a perfectly square position at impact. Head and lower body remain absolutely still through impact.

5 At the finish Head and lower body remain motionless. The head is still down.

" Half of golf is fun; the other half is putting. "
— Peter Dobereiner

Score Saver

Develop confidence: Before striking any putt, imagine watching your ball roll with perfect line and velocity as it proceeds to fall into the hole. Use this kind of visualization especially while practicing. It will pay great dividends when it comes to putting on the course.

Although there are many putting styles used by today's golf professionals, there are certain technical rules that promise success. This section will help you build these elements into your stroke. Introduce new skills one at a time—it may take several practice sessions to master each element.

Diagnosing stroke problems

The way you miss can often point to the technical fault in your stroke. Here are a few ways to diagnose problems.

Putt 10 balls

• Find a flat 10-footer and putt 10 balls at the hole. Do not watch the results. When you're finished, analyze the results using the chart below, then work on the solution in the following pages:

Location	Problem
Scattered	Inconsistency
Short left	Deceleration; aim; tentativeness
Long left	Bottom hand too dominant; aim
Short right	Deceleration; aim; tentativeness
Long right	Rushed stroke; aim; top hand too dominant; body movement

Use a chalk line

• Snap a 10-foot chalk line along a flat 10-footer. Putt balls along the line, watching where they roll in relation to the line.

Dew-covered green

• The early morning provides an excellent opportunity to recognize your putting flaws. Make several putts to a selection of different holes when the green is dew-covered. Then examine the path of the ball through the dew to see where your misses tend to roll.

Finding a Proper Grip

Getting a grip

• There are dozens of putting grips, but most are variations of the two techniques shown at right. The reverse overlap, is preferred by most pros because it helps the hands to function as a unit. Also be sure that your palms face each other and are squarely aligned with the putter face.

Score Saver

Weaken grip: One cause of pulled putts is too strong a grip, with the hands oriented too far to the right (for right-handed golfers). Through impact, this will tend to make the hands turn to the left, closing the clubface. To stop this tendency, move both hands to the left a bit. Experiment until you find something that works and feels good.

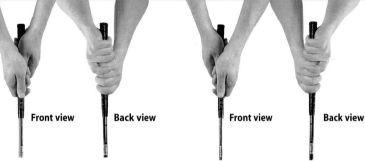

Front view **Back view**   **Front view** **Back view**

Neutral putting grip (reverse overlap)
❶ Hold the putter lightly in your left hand so the grip lies along the lifeline and the thumb is down the center of the shaft.
❷ Add the right hand so that the thumb lies along the top of the shaft. For reverse overlap, place the left index finger over one of more of the fingers of the right hand. For conventional overlap, place the right pinky between the left index and middle fingers.

Cross-handed grip
❶ Hold the putter lightly in your right hand so the grip lies along the lifeline and the thumb is oriented along the top of the shaft.
❷ Add the left hand, aligning the thumb along the top of the shaft and overlapping the right index finger over one or more fingers of the left. For conventional overlap, place the left pinky between the right index and middle fingers.

As a good golf swing follows from a good set-up, so a good putting stroke comes from a good stance and posture. Again, unless you're a great putter already, ignore the exceptions and build a solid technique. The following tips and drill will help you set up properly to putt.

Eyes over ball

• Stand so that your eyes are over the target line, regardless of your putting style. This allows for better alignment and ensures a better stroke.

Hands under shoulders

• Allows arms to swing naturally and follow a straight path.

Weight favoring forward foot

• Helps encourage a level stroke and minimizes leg movement.

Shoulders parallel to the target line

• Helps ensure a straight swing path and aids with putting alignment. Although it is not vital that the feet also be parallel, many find it helpful in order to keep the shoulders square—a must for better results.

Drop Ball Drill

Assume your normal stance, orienting your eyes over the ball and target line. To check your position, have a friend hold a ball at the bridge of your nose and drop it. The dropped ball should hit the ball you are setting up to putt. If it doesn't, adjust your stance and try the drill again.

Stroke

One of the most obvious changes in recommended putting practice in the last 40 years is the removal of the wrists from the stroke. Over the years, the best putters discovered that when the wrists are involved, there is a greater tendency for the putterhead to go off-line. The best way to ensure a square putter path is to lock the left wrist and make the stroke with just the arms and shoulders. Concentrate on keeping the putter on-line during the backswing and follow-through.

Score Saver

Imitate the best: A great way to improve your putting is to watch the best putters on tour and imitate them. Concentrate on how they read, set-up for, and stroke each putt.

At the top of the backswing, the triangle is intact, head and legs still, and wrists locked.

Impact, like set-up, finds the top of the triangle parallel to the ground,

Finish mirrors the top of the backswing. The triangle is intact, head and legs are still, and wrists remain locked.

" Why am I using a new putter? Because the last one didn't float well. "
— Craig Stadler

In the end, the putterhead alone contacts the ball and sets it rolling. It follows that if the putterhead isn't square at set-up or at impact, your putts are not going to fall. Here are tips for aligning the putterhead and keeping it square through impact.

• If you're having trouble aligning your clubhead, assume your normal putting address position and have a friend stand behind you to check your position. Then stroke a few putts as he watches so he can also check your impact position.

• Sometimes alignment may become easier with the use of visual guides. Locate a flat 6- to 8-foot putt on a practice green and lay a flag down parallel to the path to the hole. Stroke putts using the flag as a guide.

Betsy King Drill

LPGA Tour pro Betsy King checks her putterhead alignment from behind to ensure it's square before she putts. Try it on the practice green to verify your alignment.

2x4 Drill

Lay two 2x4s on the green parallel to each other and each an inch from either end of your putterhead. Stroke several putts using the boards as swing path guides. When you have the feel of a square stroke, remove them and hit some putts of similar length.

Two-Ball Drill

This drill ensures a square putterhead at impact. Place two balls on the green so they are touching one another. Mentally draw a line through the balls' centers. Stroke a putt of medium distance along the line the balls describe. If the putterhead is square at impact, both balls should follow the same path.

Keep it Quiet

The best putters keep their body very quiet through the stroke. That's because they know movement in the body, including the legs, hips, and head, will tend to cause the putterhead to go off-line.

• Monitor your feet, and be aware of any weight shift during the swing. Weight shift usually means leg movement. Try keeping most of your weight on the forward foot at address to quiet the legs. Have a friend watch or videotape you to find out if your head remains still, especially with short putts. Try this drill to reduce premature head motion.

• Place the ball on top of a quarter without noticing whether the coin is heads or tails up. Strike the ball and look down at the quarter to see whether it is heads or tails before you look at your ball rolling toward the hole.

Against the Wall Drills

These drills will help you get the feeling of stillness during the putting stroke by holding your body in a set position throughout the movement.

• Stand facing a wall and set up to putt. Lean your head against a cushion on the wall and hit several putts, feeling that your head is completely still. Then step away from the wall and try to replicate the feeling in a normal stroke.

• Now reverse the process. Set up to hit a putt with your rear end against the wall. Strike several putts, then step away and hit several from your normal stance, trying to replicate the feeling.

" Gimme: An agreement between two losers who can't putt. "
— Jim Bishop

Building Good Technique

It is difficult to control a putter when it is decelerating. If the arms slow or stop before the stroke is complete, the putterhead will tend to close, leading to pulled putts. A tentative, decelerating stroke also causes many putts to come up short.

If your stroke accelerates too quickly, your arms will get ahead of the putterhead, leading to pushed putts. A smooth, gentle acceleration is best for keeping the clubhead square and on-line. Use the following drills and tips to help promote the proper acceleration.

" It's nothing new or original to say that golf is played one stroke at a time. But it took me years to realize it. "
— Bobby Jones

Ball Behind Ball Drill

To discourage a decelerating putting stroke, place a ball several inches behind the ball you plan to putt and stroke the putt without hitting the ball on your backswing.

Shuffle Putt Drill

Here's a great drill for eliminating deceleration through the putting stroke. Set up as normal for a 2- to 3-foot putt. Without taking a backswing, push the ball forward the required distance. This will eliminate the fear of the foreswing and promote an on-line follow-through.

Keep it Smooth

Smoothness is the wild card in every golf stroke. A beautiful golf stroke is neither jerky nor quick, but seems to be preset to a perfect rhythm. Here's a simple way to find ideal rhythm and tempo: Set up to putt. Now, counting to 4 at a normal pace, stay still on your count of 1 and 2, take your backswing on 3 and make impact on 4. Try it!!

The keys to rhythm are primarily mental. Focus on soft hands, a proper follow-through, and most importantly, on visualizing the speed at which the ball will be rolling rather than the technical aspects of the stroke.

" Actually, the Lord answers my prayers everywhere except on the golf course. "
— Billy Graham

Feel the Stoke Drill and Eyes Closed Drill

These drills help develop a "feel" for the location of the hole and a trust in a non-manipulative stroke. For the feel the stroke drill, set up to hit a putt of 5 to 6 feet. Once set-up is complete, turn your head and look at the hole. Then make the stroke. Repeat the putt until you have made it several times. Then move to another location and a slightly longer putt. Repeat the exercise on putts of several different lengths. The eyes closed drill is just what it sounds like. Set up and hit putts of various lengths with eyes closed. Then guess how far your ball is from the hole before opening your eyes. This teaches a sense of how hard to hit the ball.

Score Saver

Consider the wind: A fierce wind will have an effect on the line of your putts, particularly if you are putting on fast greens. If there's a brisk wind when you arrive at the course, test its effect while putting on the practice green. As a simple adjustment, widen your stance for better stability during the stroke.

Long Putts

Long putts occasionally provide moments of glory during a round of golf. More often than not, however, they are the starting point for three-putts. Many golfers are confounded by judging distance. Others have trouble with slopes on putts that can sometimes have multiple breaks. The following section will provide tips for improving your long putts.

Tips for long putts

• Use the length of your backswing not the speed of your stroke to control distance. Rehearse the stroke, and check your follow-through: on an accelerating stroke, it should be longer than your backswing.

• On very long putts, play for a two-putt. Imagine a circle with a 3-foot radius around the hole. Aim to be inside the circle with your first putt.

• Once you've taken a read and are ready to putt, concentrate on distance.

• Don't over-practice long bombs, but try to hit a few during every practice session.

❝ Putts get difficult to read the day they hand out the money. ❞
— Lee Trevino

Right-Hand Drill

In a neutral grip, the left hand guides the putter and the right hand provides most of the force. Putting with the right hand only helps develop the feel for distance. Set up and hit putts with the right hand only. Hit putts of several different lengths until your distance control is good. Then replicate the feel with your normal grip.

Cluster Putting Drill

This is a great drill for finding the feel of various distances. Gather 8 to 10 balls on the practice green. Putt the first ball any distance, then putt the rest to the same distance. Repeat the process, putting the first ball to a different distance.

Speed and Touch Drill

Here is a another good drill for developing distance judgment. Gather several balls on the practice green. Putt the first ball approximately 10 feet. Without removing this ball, make a second putt attempting to putt it a foot past the first ball. Continue putting balls, each one foot past the previous. Repeat several times. This drill can also be done decreasing the distance of each putt.

Dealing with Slope

The long breaking putt is the toughest on any golf course. Half the problem is figuring out where to hit the ball; the other half is actually hitting it where you want to. Always take a careful read before stroking these putts. Speed should be your primary focus. Take a couple of extra practice strokes during your preshot routine to emulate the length of stroke required. Take your stance and just before you hit the putt, stand tall and scan the line of the putt one more time to get a feel for how hard to hit the ball.

" Putting is like wisdom, partly a natural gift and partly the accumulation of experience. "
— Arnold Palmer

Tips for reading greens

• Make your reading sequence a habit and repeat it every time. Observe the overall terrain and note grain, moisture and wind factors. Look at length of grass, check slope of putt from a few angles and visualize the ball going in before stepping up to hit it. Always get down low to read from behind—this allows you to best see the line and any subtle undulations. On heavy breakers, pick an intermediary target (page 17).

• If you often miss putts on the low side, allow for more break than you think. You'll probably end up making a few more putts.

Score Saver

Imagine a shorter putt: On quick downhill putts, try to imagine the force required in terms of a level putt. For example, a 10-foot downhiller may only require the same force as a 3-foot flat putt. So rather than trying to feed a 10-footer down to the hole, try picking a spot 3 feet ahead and stroke the ball with confidence.

How to plumb bob

If you're having trouble figuring out which way a putt breaks, stand behind the ball so the hole, the ball and your dominant eye are in a straight line. Set your body perpendicular to the slope and hold your putter so it hangs vertically and covers the ball. Close your non-dominant eye. The putt will break toward the side the hole appears on.

Score Saver

Make your own decisions: Generally, no two players perceive the same putt in exactly the same way. One might play less break and more speed, while another will allow for a lot of movement on a slower putt. All this is to say that watching the putts of playing partners in order to get a read might not be as useful as you think. Once you have enough experience, trusting your own judgment is usually best. If you are truly undecided, go ahead and try to glean information from the putts of other players.

See the Line Drill

This is a great drill for developing the ability to visualize break. Set up over a severely sloping putt. Stroke several balls until you've made it and are comfortable visualizing the break. Repeat the exercise on several other sloping putts to the same hole. Then move to another hole and repeat the process.

Spot-Putting Drill

When faced with a breaking putt, most players become too concerned with the hole itself and tend to underplay the break. To eliminate this tendency, set up for a hard-breaking putt and choose a spot about 2 feet along the intended pathway. Try to roll the ball with correct speed over this spot. Adjust the spot as necessary to hole the putt. Repeat on several breaking putts.

Short Putts

It's a well-known golf truism that a 2-foot putt counts for as much as a 300-yard drive. But too often golfers devote little time to this part of the game. One of the quickest ways to lower your scores is to become proficient at holing short putts. The following tips should help you hole the shorts ones.

18

Score Saver

Observe around the hole: The area around the hole receives more foot traffic than any other part of the green. Sparse grass, ball marks, spike and scuff marks and other indentations caused by walking can seriously affect the roll of a putt. It is against the rules to repair spike marks, but you may repair all ball-marks in the area. Take the condition of the ground into account when you putt. Whether you have a long or short putt, you may need to adjust your speed and line to give yourself a better chance of making it.

Tips for short putts

- Stroke the ball firmly and have a positive attitude. Nothing causes more short-putt agony than tentativeness. Remember, you can't lag a short putt.

- Let your putterhead do the work. Golfers often miss short putts because they try to guide the ball into the hole rather than making a good putting stroke. Pick a line, then concentrate on making the ball hit the back of the hole. Speed is less relevant on short putts than direction.

- Don't give the hole away. Unless you see a truly severe break, most short putts should be played inside the hole.
- Always assume a solid stance and feel balanced before you strike a putt. You may need to widen your stance in severe wind.
- Exaggerate your follow-through on-line.

" I don't fear death, but I sure do hate those three-footers for par. **"**
— Chi Chi Rodriguez

Score Saver

Use your ball logo to align putter path: To help keep your stroke on-line, align the logo on the ball in the direction of the putter path you want to follow. As you make your stroke, imagine stroking along the path it describes.

Putt to a Tee Drill

This drill will make the cup appear larger than it really is. Place a tee in the ground on the practice green. Putt to it with several balls from a variety of angles, attempting to hit it at the proper speed each time. After succeeding at this several times, remove the tee and putt at the hole normally. The hole will appear to be larger, and your confidence will increase as a result.

Distance and Direction Drill

This is a great drill for learning feel for short putts and building confidence. Place six to eight balls each a foot apart in a straight line leading away from the hole. Putt them in in order, starting with the shortest putt.

Clamp Grip Drill

PGA star Bernhard Langer used this grip to try to put an end to his short-putting woes, and for a while it worked. It's a great drill for developing solid wrists through the stroke. Hold the putter with your left hand down the grip. With your right hand, clamp the putter against the inside of your left forearm. Hit a number of putts this way, then go back to your normal grip.

Hover the Putterhead Drill

Missed short putts often result from a putter path that cuts across the line of the putt. Check your putter path by laying down a club and hovering your putter above the path. Make several strokes, checking the path with the shaft. Repeat until your path is in line with the shaft.

Score Saver

Know your style: Putting styles fall into two broad camps—the chargers and the diers. Chargers aim to hit the back of the cup, so the cup traps the ball. They attack the hole with confidence. Arnold Palmer was a famous charge-putter. Diers aim to drop the ball just over the front edge of the cup. If the putt is on-line, it drops in. If not, it may still drop in the side. Both strategies have their devotees. The key is to discover which type you are and stick with it. Knowing your style will allow you to work on it and develop consistency on the greens.

" The only thing a golfer needs is more daylight. **"**
— Ben Hogan

The Dreaded Yips

A golfer who agonizes over short putts, and misses a good many of them, is said to have "the yips." Those who have them seem to be under some kind of curse that destroys confidence and coordination. The following ideas and mental tips might help.

• Take the pressure off. Stop talking to yourself. Likely much of what you're saying is negative.

• Do not wait over the putt too long. Step up with a plan and stroke the putt.

• Develop a new putt position or posture, or try a different putter.

• Use visual imagery. Listen, don't look for the putt to drop.

Reason to celebrate
Sometimes a change in grip, posture or equipment helps change the pattern enough to send the yips packing.

Watch the Date on the Quarter Drill

Golfers with the yips need to stop focusing on making putts and simply try to make good putting strokes. This drill will help keep focus off results. Set up as normal for a short putt, but place a quarter under your ball. Make a normal stroke, but as you move through impact, concentrate on reading the date on the quarter. This will take focus off the hole, and probably help you relax over short putts.

Tips for Practice

Few golfers can devote the time they'd like to practice. On the occasions when they are free, they'd rather play. But, practice is critical to improving. This is as true for putting as for any other part of the game. These pages provide strategies to help you make the most of your practice time.

22

Too many golfers hit the practice green and start rolling the long bombs. It's a good idea to hit a few, but spend more time on putts from that are 2 to 12 feet in length. It's there that your score will more likely be decided. Practice a variety of short and medium-length putts with different

Score Saver

Hit the green first: Before playing, golfers typically head first to the practice tee, often leaving little time for putting and chipping. There are two reasons to reverse this order. First, on average, more than 50% of strokes are taken on or around the green. Second, putting and chipping provides a gradual warm-up before taking full swings.

breaks, as well as uphill and downhill slopes. Don't forget, confidence in your short putting will spill over into your long putts and short game. You'll be more relaxed over a 30-footer or a tough chip if you know you have a decent chance of making any second putt within a reasonable distance. Finally, you'll learn better if you're challenging yourself and having fun. Try the games on the opposite page to make your putting practice time more enjoyable.

❝ Practice puts brains in your muscles. ❞
— Sam Snead

Putting Tips

Golfers spend almost 50% of their strokes on putts. This On the Go guide, with its techniques and strategies developed by top USGTF teachers, will help you knock that number down. Tips and drills deal with long putts, short putts, and reading breaks.

Choosing a Putter
Putter styles

The Putting Stroke
Swing sequence

Building Good Technique
Proper grip · Correct posture · Stroke

Long Putts
Dealing with slope · Drills

Short Putts
The dreaded yips · Drills

Tips for Practice
Practice games

ACKNOWLEDGMENTS:
Mark Harman, Course Director, USGTF; David Hill, CPGA, The Golfologist Academy; Mario Pepin, Golf Chuck Brown; Les Installations Sportive Defargo, www.defargo.com

For more great ideas and essential information, visit us at
onthegoguides.com
or call us at 1-866-616-4040

© 2002, St. Remy Media Inc.
Printed in Korea

ISBN 1-894827-20-1
9 781894 827201

Practice Games

Great putters can invariably tell stories about their marathon practice sessions. Most often, some kind of competition was involved. Nothing makes the time pass more quickly or sharpens skills than competition—against yourself or someone else.

Spoke Drill

This drill helps develop skill for short putts. Choose a hole on a slope. Set up balls around it so they appear like the spokes of a wheel. Start at any ball, and go around the circle, sinking each putt. Start at a distance of 2 feet, and repeat the drill at increasing distances from the hole.

Games for the Practice Green

• **18 holes:** Two to four players. One chooses a hole, and all play to it. Par is set at 2. The player with the honor chooses the next hole. Low 18-hole score wins.

• **Horseshoes:** Two to four players. Name a hole and play to it. Sinking putt is worth 3 points. Closest to hole is worth a point. Play until a player gets 40 points.

• **Reverse stymie:** At least two players (but more is better). All players putt once and leave their balls in play. After all first putts are hit, assess distance from hole. Closest to hole hits second putt first, attempting to hole out. Next closest player hits second putt, and so on. All players must leave their balls as they lie until everyone has hit their second putts. All players must hole out—in as few putts as possible. Even if a player doesn't sink a putt, leaving a ball close to the hole so that it 'stymies' other players is almost as good. Here's how to score each hole: A hole-out counts as 0, a two-putt 2, and so on. A ball striking another ball is a 2-stroke penalty; if it hits two balls, it's 4 strokes and so on. Putting off the green is a 2-stroke penalty. The player with the lowest score on a hole plays first on next hole. Players can even push down on ball to attempt to 'jump' another ball, if necessary. Play continues for preset number of holes; lowest score wins.